Dinosaurs and Prehistoric Animals

Diplodocus

by Janet Riehecky

Consulting Editor: Gail Saunders-Smith, PhD

Consultant: Jack Horner, Curator of Paleontology
Museum of the Rockies
Bozeman, Montana

Capstone
press

Mankato, Minnesota

Pebble Plus is published by Capstone Press,
151 Good Counsel Drive, P.O. Box 669, Mankato, Minnesota 56002.
www.capstonepress.com

1 2 3 4 5 6 11 10 09 08 07 06

Library of Congress Cataloging-in-Publication Data
Riehecky, Janet, 1953–
    Diplodocus / by Janet Riehecky.
    p. cm.—(Pebble plus. Dinosaurs and prehistoric animals)
    Summary: "Simple text and illustrations present the life of diplodocus, how it looked, and its
behavior"—Provided by publisher.
    Includes bibliographical references and index.
    ISBN-13: 978-0-7368-5352-1 (hardcover)
    ISBN-10: 0-7368-5352-9 (hardcover)
    1. Diplodocus—Juvenile literature. I. Title. II. Series.
QE862.S3R5356 2006
567.913—dc22   2005020796

Editorial Credits
Sarah L. Schuette, editor; Linda Clavel, designer; Wanda Winch, photo researcher

Illustration and Photo Credits
Jon Hughes, illustrator
Thomas R. Wilcox, 21

The author dedicates this book to her niece Sarah.

Note to Parents and Teachers

The Dinosaurs and Prehistoric Animals set supports national science standards related
to the evolution of life. This book describes and illustrates diplodocus. The images
support early readers in understanding the text. The repetition of words and phrases
helps early readers learn new words. This book also introduces early readers to subject-
specific vocabulary words, which are defined in the Glossary section. Early readers may
need assistance to read some words and to use the Table of Contents, Glossary, Read
More, Internet Sites, and Index sections of the book.

Table of Contents

diplodocus (dip-LOH-doh-kus)

A Spiky Dinosaur

Diplodocus had a long neck
and a long tail.
It had spikes on its back.

Diplodocus lived
in prehistoric times.
It lived in western
North America about
150 million years ago.

How Diplodocus Looked

Diplodocus was as long as three fire trucks. It was about 90 feet (27 meters) long.

Diplodocus had

four thick legs.

Diplodocus was so big

that it walked very slowly.

Diplodocus had
a very long tail.
Its tail looked like a whip.

Diplodocus had
short teeth shaped like pegs.
It stripped leaves from plants
that grew close
to the ground.

What Diplodocus Did

Female diplodocuses

laid their eggs

while they walked.

The eggs landed safely

on the ground.

Diplodocuses traveled

in groups.

They protected their young

from other dinosaurs.

The End of Diplodocus

Diplodocuses died

about 145 million years ago.

No one knows why

they all died.

You can see diplodocus

fossils in museums.

Glossary

dinosaur—a large reptile that lived on land in prehistoric times

fossil—the remains or traces of an animal or a plant

museum—a place where objects of art, history, or science are shown

prehistoric—very, very old; prehistoric means belonging to a time before history was written down.

protect—to keep safe

whip—a long, thin piece of leather

Read More

Cohen, Daniel. *Diplodocus.* Discovering Dinosaurs. Mankato, Minn.: Bridgestone Books, 2003.

Dahl, Michael. *Double Bones: The Adventure of Diplodocus.* Dinosaur World. Minneapolis: Picture Window Books, 2005.

Skrepnick, Michael William. *Diplodocus—Gigantic Long-Necked Dinosaur.* I Like Dinosaurs! Berkeley Heights, N.J.: Enslow, 2005.

Internet Sites

FactHound offers a safe, fun way to find Internet sites related to this book. All of the sites on FactHound have been researched by our staff.

Here's how:

1. Visit *www.facthound.com*

2. Type in this special code **0736853529** for age-appropriate sites. Or enter a search word related to this book for a more general search.

3. Click on the **Fetch It** button.

FactHound will fetch the best sites for you!

Index

Word Count: 138
Grade: 1
Early-Intervention Level: 12